SPEAK *life* TO CHANGE YOUR *life*

Harnessing the Power of Personalized Scripture Confessions

MyVersion LLC.

Speak Life to Change Your Life

Harnessing the Power of Personalized
Scripture Confessions

Print Edition
ISBN 13: 979-8-89846-000-6
Copyright © 2025 MyVersion LLC.

Published by MyVersion LLC.
https://MyVersionBook.com

Contents

Introduction

Words carry tremendous power. From the earliest pages of Scripture, we see that God created the heavens and the earth with His spoken word (Genesis 1:1-3). He did not silently think the universe into being; He spoke it into existence. This foundational truth reveals an important spiritual principle: <u>spoken words release creative power</u>. As beings made in God's image (Genesis 1:26-27), our words likewise carry a force that can shape our lives, our futures, and our interactions with the world around us.

This booklet explores the transforming power of faith-filled confessions, especially when they are personalized from Scripture. By "confession," we do not only mean the acknowledgment of sins or shortcomings—though that is an important spiritual discipline (1 John 1:9). Here, we refer to the deliberate, faith-filled speaking of God's Word over our circumstances, mindsets, health, and every aspect of life. This practice is rooted in biblical truths about the authority of the believer, the creative power of our words, and the goodness of God who desires to see His children walk in blessing, victory, and the fullness of His promises.

In the following pages, we will investigate the scriptural foundation for speaking faith-filled confessions. We will learn about the importance of aligning our words with the truths of Scripture, the significance of renewing our minds, and the practical steps to living a lifestyle of victory. This booklet seeks to illuminate the principle that faith is activated through the spoken word. When you learn to put God's promises on your lips, you will release His power to transform your life from the inside out.

May this teaching strengthen your faith and encourage you to personalize the promises of God so that you can witness the magnificent results of living a life dedicated to faith in His Word.

Chapter 1
The Foundation of Faith

Faith in God's Word

From the outset, we must recognize that faith cannot exist independently of God's Word. Romans 10:17 declares, "So then faith comes by hearing, and hearing by the word of God." If our desire is to grow in faith, the most direct path is through immersing ourselves in

Scripture and letting it guide our thoughts, shape our beliefs, and inform our speech.

It's worth mentioning that according to John 1:1, God is the Word, and the Word is God. Truly the quickest way to getting God's results, is through the Word.

The beauty of biblical faith is that it never rests on wishful thinking or vague hope. It has a solid foundation in God's promises. Hebrews 11:1 describes faith as "the substance of things hoped for, the evidence of things not seen." To live by faith is to confidently trust that God's Word is true—no matter what our natural circumstances appear to be. This confidence then shapes what we choose to speak and believe about our situations.

The Power of Belief and Confession

Belief in the heart, accompanied by confession with the mouth, is a central principle of the Christian life. Romans 10:9-10 explains that the road to salvation involves believing in one's heart and confessing with one's mouth that Jesus is Lord. Although that scripture specifically speaks to the salvation experience, it reveals a powerful truth about how kingdom realities are activated: <u>believing in the heart and speaking with the mouth.</u>

Belief does not remain a private, hidden matter. It finds expression in what we say. Throughout Scripture, we see examples of men and women whose declarations—rooted in their trust in God—unleashed divine intervention. David declared to Goliath in 1 Samuel 17:46, "This day the Lord will deliver you into my hand." Though David was physically smaller and less equipped in the natural, he believed in his heart and spoke words aligned with that faith. He then acted on what he declared and saw God bring victory.

Likewise, we are encouraged to wield the "sword of the Spirit, which is the word of God" (Ephesians 6:17). This is not merely knowledge of the Bible but its active, spoken application. <u>Faith, then, is both what we embrace in our hearts and the words we release from our mouths.</u>

The Example of Abraham

An outstanding example of faith in God's Word is Abraham. Romans 4:17 (NKJV) quotes God as saying, "I have made you a father of many nations," and describes that God "calls those things which do not exist as though they did." Although Abraham was old and childless, he chose to trust in the promise of God rather than the apparent impossibility of his situation. He began living in the reality of that promise long before Isaac was born.

This is not pretending we don't have a problem. It is not denying reality. Rather, it is acknowledging a higher reality—that God's Word stands above all else. If we desire to see life-changing transformation, we must imitate this biblical pattern. We look at Scripture, see what it declares about our situation, and speak in agreement with it, even before we see any changes in the natural.

Faith as the Substance

Faith is the "substance of things hoped for" (Hebrews 11:1). In other words, faith brings into the present the realities we anticipate. When we personalize and declare scripture-based promises, we are not merely rehearsing positive phrases; <u>we are cooperating with the creative power of God's Word to bring forth His will in our lives.</u>

This foundation sets the stage for under-standing why speaking personalized, faith-filled confessions is so vital. It is not a formula or a ritual to make us feel better momentarily. It is an act of partnership with the living God, who invites us to participate in His redemptive work in our own lives and, ultimately, in the world.

Chapter 2
The Creative Power of the Tongue

Life and Death Are in the Tongue

One of the most direct statements about the power of words is found in Proverbs 18:21: "Death and life are in the power of the tongue." That should give us pause. Scripture explicitly states that our words hold the power to bring forth either life or death. This potency is built into the very fabric of how God created humanity.

Throughout the Bible, we encounter stories illustrating the impact of spoken words. In Joshua 6, God instructed Joshua to have the people remain silent for six days as they marched around Jericho, and then on the seventh day, they were to shout. That shout—together with their obedience—brought down the fortified walls of Jericho. Their voices, combined with faith and obedience, became the conduit for divine power.

Aligning Our Words with God's Word

If we want to walk in the fullness of what God has provided, we must align our words with

His Word. Jesus taught that "out of the abundance of the heart the mouth speaks" (Matthew 12:34). Thus, what we fill our hearts with will eventually come out of our mouths. <u>If our hearts are saturated in Scripture, our spoken words will reflect God's perspective, bringing life-giving outcomes.</u>

Conversely, if our hearts are full of fear, unbelief, or negativity, our words will reflect that condition, and we may inadvertently speak destructive outcomes into our lives. James 3:6 compares the tongue to a fire, warning that careless speech can set our entire life ablaze with negative consequences. When we use our words to agree with fear or the enemy's lies, we open the door for those realities to manifest.

Mark 11 and Mountain-Moving Faith

A hallmark passage on speaking faith-filled words is found in Mark 11:22-24. Here, Jesus encourages His disciples to "Have faith in God," or as some translations note, "Have the faith of God." He continues, saying, "whoever says to this mountain, 'Be removed and be cast into the sea,' and does not doubt in his heart but believes … he will have whatever he says" (v. 23). Notice that Jesus emphasizes speaking to the mountain, not merely thinking about it, complaining about it, or wishing it away. He instructs us to talk directly to the obstacle with faith-filled words based on God's promise.

This teaching underscores the direct link between believing in our hearts and speaking with our mouths. When confronting life's mountains—be they sickness, financial lack, strained relationships, or mental oppression—we are to respond as Jesus taught: speak to that mountain with faith in God. <u>It is not our human authority that moves the mountain, but the authority of God's Word on our lips.</u>

A Guard Over the Mouth

In Psalm 141:3, the psalmist prays, "Set a guard, O Lord, over my mouth; keep watch over the door of my lips." Recognizing the weightiness of our words should drive us to ask God for help in ensuring our speech lines up with truth, grace, and divine wisdom. <u>A disciplined tongue, surrendered to the Holy</u>

Spirit, becomes a powerful instrument for releasing life into every situation. As we internalize and speak Scripture, we position ourselves to see God's miraculous power manifested in our everyday lives.

Chapter 3
Renewing the Mind through Confession

The Battle for the Mind

Although words carry creative power, they are shaped by our mindsets and beliefs. Romans 12:2 exhorts us to "be transformed by the renewing of your mind." This transformation process involves displacing worldly, negative, or fear-based thought patterns with God's truth.

Speaking personalized Scripture confessions is one of the most effective ways to renew our minds. When we repeatedly declare God's promises, these truths begin to take root in our thought life. They dislodge the lies and establish a new worldview based on the Bible rather than natural circumstances.

Meditation and Confession Go Hand in Hand

Joshua 1:8 provides a timeless key to success: "This Book of the Law shall not depart from your mouth, but you shall meditate in it day and night … for then you will make your way prosperous, and then you will have good success." Notice that it does not say to meditate silently alone. Rather, the text emphasizes that the Word should "not depart from your mouth." The Hebrew word for "meditate" includes the sense of muttering or speaking softly, indicating that biblical meditation involves speaking the Word in a reflective, worshipful manner.

<u>As you speak scripture confessions, you engage not just your intellect but your entire being—spirit, soul, and body.</u> Through consistent confession, Scripture's truths move from head knowledge to heart revelation. Once anchored in the heart, those truths will naturally influence every area of life, producing blessing and success in alignment with God's will.

Tearing Down Strongholds

Second Corinthians 10:4-5 explains that we use spiritual weapons to pull down strong-holds—wrong patterns of thinking that exalt themselves against the knowledge of God. Negative habits of thinking might have been built over years of hearing and believing misinformation or harmful lies about ourselves or about God's nature.

Through the power of the Word, spoken in faith, these strongholds can be dismantled. As you continue to declare, "I have the mind of Christ" (1 Corinthians 2:16), "I can do all things through Christ who strengthens me" (Philippians 4:13), or "The Lord is my shepherd; I shall not want" (Psalm 23:1), your soul (mind, will, and emotions) begins to align with the truth. The lies become exposed, and your perspective changes, allowing the Holy Spirit to transform your thinking.

Aligning Our Desires with God's

When our minds are renewed, we begin to desire what God desires, think as He thinks, and speak as He speaks. When Jesus taught His disciples to pray, "Your kingdom come. Your will be done on earth as it is in heaven" (Matthew 6:10), He was instructing them to align their words and heart posture with God's heavenly purposes. The renewed mind, saturated with Scripture, naturally releases prayer, worship, and declarations that harmonize with heaven's perspective.

This chapter emphasizes that speaking faith-filled confessions is not mere wishful thinking or an empty formula. Rather, <u>it is a divine process that renews our minds and positions us to experience the fullness of God's good and perfect will in every area of life.</u>

Chapter 4
Personalized Scripture for Your Life

Why Personalization Matters

Confessing Scripture gains extraordinary power when it is personalized. It is one thing to say, "God so loved the world," and quite another to say, "God so loved me that He gave His only Son for my salvation and wholeness." Personalization bridges the gap between a general statement and a heart-level revelation. It allows the Holy Spirit to breathe life into the Word, making it specific to your unique situation.

When Jesus declared in Luke 4:18-19, "The Spirit of the Lord is upon Me," He was quoting Isaiah's prophecy about the Messiah. By applying that scripture to Himself, He revealed that He had taken ownership of the Word's promise. This act of personalized confession unveiled the truth of His identity and mission.

Likewise, the moment we personalize God's promises, we affirm, "This is who I am in Christ. This is my inheritance. This is God's will for me." Such confessions cultivate a sense of holy confidence because they remind us that God's promises are not for others alone, but for us individually.

Practical Examples of Personalization

Consider the passage in Ephesians 1:3, which says, "Blessed be the God and Father of our Lord Jesus Christ, who has blessed us with every spiritual blessing in Christ." You could personalize this to say, "Thank You, Father, that You have blessed me with every spiritual blessing in Christ. I declare that I have favor, wisdom, and everything I need to fulfill Your purpose for my life today."

By using personal pronouns and present-tense verbs, you engage your heart in active faith.

Another example is from the well-known passage from Psalm 23.

You might read, "The Lord is my Shepherd; I shall not want," but in confession form, you can say, "The Lord is my Shepherd; I do not lack any good thing today. He leads me to green pastures and still waters. He restores my soul."

<u>Such personalization turns a broad truth into a dynamic, faith-building declaration.</u>

Speaking to Specific Areas of Your Life

The Word of God addresses every domain of life—finances, health, relationships, emotional well-being, and beyond. Rather than using generalized statements, you can craft your confessions to tackle particular concerns. For instance, if you face sickness, you might declare, "By His stripes I am healed" (Isaiah 53:5; 1 Peter 2:24). If you are dealing with anxiety, you might proclaim, "God has not given me a spirit of fear, but of power and of love and of a sound mind" (2 Timothy 1:7).

Targeting specific areas with Scripture-based confessions makes your faith more purposeful. It also empowers you to recognize and resist any form of unbelief or contradiction that may arise. When negative thoughts attempt to creep in, you can counter them with the truth you have previously spoken.

Writing Down Your Confessions or Reading them on Paper

One effective method to keep yourself consistent is to write down your personalized confessions or get a book with your name inserted into the scriptures. When you see them on paper (or in digital form), it is easier to remember them and speak them consistently. You can then review and revise them as the Holy Spirit leads, ensuring your confessions remain relevant to your current season of life.

<u>By personalizing Scripture and making it your own, you are actively participating in the practice of proclaiming God's truth</u>. This approach not only transforms the mind but also sets the stage for witnessing the tangible

manifestation of God's promises in every area of your life.

Chapter 5
Overcoming Obstacles with Bold Declarations

The Reality of Spiritual Opposition

Scripture teaches that we have an adversary who seeks to steal, kill, and destroy (John 10:10; 1 Peter 5:8). However, we are also assured that the power of the enemy cannot prevail against believers who stand in the authority of Christ (Luke 10:19). One of the most powerful ways to enforce this victory is through bold, faith-filled declarations of God's Word.

When Jesus was tempted in the wilderness (Matthew 4:1-11), He did not simply endure the barrage of temptation in silence. Instead, He consistently countered the devil's words with the written Word of God, saying, "It is written…" Each time, the enemy's attempts were dismantled by Jesus' verbal proclamation of truth. As followers of Christ, we are called to do likewise.

Identifying Your Mountains

In Mark 11:23, Jesus specifically mentions speaking to the mountain. A "mountain" can represent any large, seemingly immovable obstacle—whether it's a financial crisis, a

chronic health condition, a broken relationship, or a deeply entrenched habit. The first
step is identifying that mountain in the light of
God's Word, recognizing how it opposes His
promises for your life.

Armed with Scripture that addresses your
situation, you begin to speak directly to that
obstacle. For instance, if your mountain is
financial lack, you might declare verses such
as Philippians 4:19, "My God shall supply all
my need according to His riches in glory by
Christ Jesus," or Deuteronomy 8:18, "God
gives me the power to get wealth." You then
speak to lack, commanding it to depart and
declaring your alignment with God's
provision.

Overcoming Fear and Doubt

In the process of speaking to your mountains, you might grapple with fear, uncertainty, or doubt. Such emotions are natural responses to adverse circumstances, but they should not dictate your final stance. Second Corinthians 4:13 tells us, "And since we have the same spirit of faith … we also believe and therefore speak." Faith is a spiritual force that transcends fleeting emotions. <u>By continuing to speak God's Word in the face of adversity, you signal your trust in His character, not in your own ability or circumstances.</u>

Our adversary will often attempt to sow doubt, whispering, "It's not working," or, "You're being unrealistic." Counter these thoughts with Scripture. As James 4:7 instructs, "Resist the devil and he will flee from you." That resistance includes both standing firm in your convictions and verbally rejecting any falsehood that tries to exalt itself above God's truth.

Testimonies of Victory

Throughout Scripture, countless individuals overcame insurmountable odds through faith and obedience. The walls of Jericho fell, the giant Goliath was slain, the prophet Elijah called down fire from heaven, and the apostle Paul survived shipwrecks and persecutions— all by standing firmly on God's Word. Their stories are a testament to the fact that impossible situations can be conquered by those who dare to believe and speak in agreement with God.

As you adopt the same stance, you will begin to see breakthroughs in your own life. Mountains once thought immovable can become stepping stones to deeper faith, stronger character, and a greater demonstration of God's goodness.

Chapter 6
Building a Lifestyle of Victory

Consistency and Endurance

<u>Walking in victory through faith-filled confessions is not a one-time event. Just as any skill requires practice and consistency</u>, so does the discipline of aligning our words with God's Word. Galatians 6:9 exhorts us not to grow weary in doing good, for we will reap a harvest at the proper time if we do not give

up. Part of "doing good" includes consistently sowing seeds of God's promises through our speech.

When we begin to see small victories, it is crucial to continue speaking Scripture over our circumstances. Faith is a lifestyle, not merely a crisis response. Habits—both positive and negative—are built through repetition. As we repeatedly declare God's truth, it becomes second nature, and our lives begin to reflect kingdom realities more and more.

Speaking During Good Times and Challenging Times

It is often easier to maintain a faith confession when everything is going well. However, real growth happens when we continue to declare God's goodness even in trials. Paul and Silas prayed and sang hymns to God from a prison cell (Acts 16:25). Their choice to exalt God's Word over their dire circumstances led to a miraculous jailbreak that served as a powerful testimony of the gospel.

Similarly, you may find that the greatest moments to deepen your faith confession are precisely when circumstances look bleak. Rather than letting fear or discouragement define your language, you can affirm, "God is for me, who can be against me?" (Romans 8:31). This posture of unshakable trust in God allows His supernatural power to shine through.

The Importance of Thanksgiving and Praise

Philippians 4:6-7 emphasizes that our prayers and requests should be accompanied by thanksgiving. Gratitude is a powerful ally to faith. When we express our thanks to God for His promises—even before they visibly manifest—we demonstrate genuine trust.

Thanksgiving also serves to remind us of past victories and answered prayers, which further bolsters our faith for the present challenge. The psalmist repeatedly recalls God's past faithfulness as a means to encourage his soul to hope in God (Psalm 42:5). As you incorporate thanksgiving and praise into your confessions, your heart remains focused on

God's character rather than the magnitude of
the obstacle.

Living Out Your Confessions

Faith without corresponding actions is
incomplete (James 2:20). Once you have
spoken God's promises, continue to walk
them out through wise decisions and Spirit-led
steps. For example, if you are declaring that
God supplies all your needs, ask Him for
guidance on your finances and follow the
promptings of the Holy Spirit regarding wise
stewardship or generosity. If you speak
healing over your body, cooperate with that
confession by caring for your health in
practical ways.

In this manner, <u>your faith confessions become the engine that drives a lifestyle of obedience, ensuring that your beliefs and words are demonstrated through tangible actions.</u>

Chapter 7
Practical Steps for Effective Faith Confessions

Step 1: Identify the Need or Promise

Start by identifying the specific need, challenge, or desire you have. Then, find Scripture that addresses that area. This can involve using a concordance, an online search, or a study Bible to discover relevant promises.

For instance, if you need healing, look up verses on divine health and wholeness (e.g., Isaiah 53:4-5; Matthew 8:17; 1 Peter 2:24).

Step 2: Personalize the Scriptures

Rewrite or find a format where the verses are listed in a first-person declaration form, speaking them as if they were already manifest in your life. For example, "Surely, Jesus has borne my sicknesses and carried my pains, and by His stripes, I am healed." This personalization ensures that you actively engage your heart rather than reading the verses passively.

If you're looking for a quick and effective way to obtain personalized Scripture confessions, consider visiting our website at:

MyVersionBook.com. Our personalized topical confession mini-books allow you to see your name woven into the promises, providing a powerful tool for speaking God's Word over your life with greater clarity and conviction.

Step 3: Speak Regularly and Consistently

Set aside dedicated times each day to speak out your confessions—morning, midday, and evening, if possible. Consistency is crucial. Much like planting seeds in a garden, you do not see the harvest overnight. But as you keep speaking and watering the seeds with faith, the results will come.

Step 4: Guard Your Heart and Mouth

Be vigilant about words of doubt or negativity that try to slip into your speech. Remind yourself that death and life are in the power of the tongue (Proverbs 18:21). If you do slip up and speak negatively, quickly repent and reaffirm God's Word. Over time, you will find that your vocabulary naturally adjusts to reflect the truths you are standing on.

Step 5: Couple Your Confessions with Prayer and Praise

Prayer is an intimate time of fellowship with God, where we can pour out our hearts and listen to His guidance. Praise shifts our focus onto God's goodness and strengthens our faith. By combining faith confessions with prayer and praise, you cultivate an atmosphere where God's power can move freely.

Step 6: Expect Results in God's Timing

Biblical faith always involves a confident expectation that God is faithful to His Word. Hebrews 10:23 encourages us to "hold fast the confession of our hope without wavering, for He who promised is faithful." We do not always see results instantly, but we trust God's perfect timing. As we remain steadfast, we position ourselves to receive the fullness of His promises.

Chapter 8
Practical Examples of Effective Faith Confessions

Below are a few model confessions taken from various parts of Scripture. Use these as inspiration to develop your own, tailored to your current season of life.

1. Identity in Christ

"I am a new creation in Christ (2 Corinthians 5:17). The old has passed away, and all things in me have become new. I am the righteousness of God in Christ Jesus (2 Corinthians 5:21), cleansed by His blood and filled with His Spirit."

2. Healing and Health

"Jesus took my infirmities and bore my sicknesses (Matthew 8:17). By His stripes, I am healed (1 Peter 2:24). The same Spirit who raised Jesus from the dead dwells in me, and He gives life to my mortal body (Romans 8:11). I walk in divine health all my days."

3. Provision and Abundance

"My God supplies all my needs according to His riches in glory by Christ Jesus (Philippians 4:19). I am blessed coming in and blessed going out (Deuteronomy

28:6). Everything I set my hand to prospers (Psalm 1:3). I have abundance to give to every good work (2 Corinthians 9:8)."

4. Peace and Emotional Well-Being

"God has not given me a spirit of fear, but of power, love, and a sound mind (2 Timothy 1:7). The peace of God, which surpasses all understanding, guards my heart and mind in Christ Jesus (Philippians 4:7). I cast all my cares upon the Lord, for He cares for me (1 Peter 5:7)."

5. Guidance and Wisdom

"The Lord directs my steps (Proverbs 16:9). I trust in Him with all my heart, and He makes my paths straight (Proverbs 3:5-6). I have the mind of Christ (1

Corinthians 2:16), and I hear the voice of the Good Shepherd (John 10:27). I follow His leading in all I do."

By consistently declaring such confessions and others like them, you embed God's Word into your heart and actively release His power into every aspect of your life.

Conclusion
Embracing a Lifestyle of Faith-Filled Speech

Throughout this booklet, we have examined the biblical foundation for speaking personalized, faith-filled confessions. From the very start of Genesis—where God spoke creation into being—to Jesus' teaching in Mark 11:22-24 about speaking directly to mountains, the message is clear: when our words are aligned with God's will, they hold remarkable power to influence the world around us.

We also discovered that confession works hand in hand with belief. According to Romans 10:9-10, we believe in our hearts and confess with our mouths to receive salvation. By the same principle, we apply God's Word to every other area of life. As we meditate on Scripture, renew our minds, and personalize His promises, our hearts overflow with faith-filled words. These confessions then transform our attitudes, equip us to overcome obstacles, and empower us to walk victoriously in all aspects of our lives.

It is essential to remember that speaking Scripture confessions is not a magical formula or an effort to coerce God. Instead, it is a covenant principle that honors Him by taking Him at His Word and rejecting all doubt. By combining our declarations with prayer, thanksgiving, and faithful action, we deepen our relationship with Him and learn to trust Him more each day.

May the truths presented in this booklet inspire you to stand firmly on God's promises, experience breakthrough in long-standing challenges, and foster a resilient faith in the One who is "able to do exceedingly abundantly above all that we ask or think" (Ephesians 3:20). As you cultivate the habit of daily speaking God's Word, you will discover that His grace is sufficient, His power is made perfect in weakness (2 Corinthians 12:9), and His promises will never fail (Joshua 21:45).

Embrace this lifestyle of faith-filled speech and watch as your life is transformed—spirit, soul, and body—through honoring God by declaring His truth and stepping into the inheritance He has so freely given. Keep going, secure in the knowledge that His Word is "alive and powerful, sharper than any two-edged sword" (Hebrews 4:12). May you experience His boundless love, abundant provision, and mighty power as you stand on His Word and boldly speak it over your life.

We want to remind you, if you are looking to strengthen your confession practice or need help applying God's Word to specific areas of your life, consider visiting our website at MyVersionBook.com. You will find a variety of topical Scripture confession books, each personalized to include your own name, which can be a powerful catalyst in making these promises come alive in your daily walk.

MyVersion LLC.

MyVersion Publishing is the industry leading publisher for personalized scripture confession books designed to deepen your faith. Available on Amazon.com or on the web at MyVersionBook.com, our mini-books are a convenient 4x6 inch pocket sized paperback, ebook, audiobook, or Kindle; perfect for gift-giving or keeping in your pocket as a source of encouragement wherever you go.

Each book is tailored to specific topics like healing, peace from anxiety, finances, identity in Christ, and more; offering a personal touch that transforms scripture into a deeply meaningful experience.

By incorporating your name directly into the Scripture, MyVersion makes God's Word feel uniquely yours, helping you or your loved ones connect with faith on a whole new level.

Visit our website now to get your personalized books! https://MyVersionBook.com

With long life will I satisfy **Rick** and show **him** My salvation.

— *Psalm* 91:16

Jesus personally bore **Rick's** sins in His own body on the tree as on an altar and offered Himself on it, that **Rick** might die to sin and live to righteousness. By His wounds and lashes **Rick** has been healed.

— *1 Peter* 2:24

Christ purchased **Rick's** freedom redeeming **him** from the curse of the Law and its condemnation by Himself becoming a curse for **Rick**, for it is written, cursed is everyone who hangs on a tree (is crucified);

— *Galatians* 3:13

www.ingramcontent.com/pod-product-compliance
Lightning Source LLC
Chambersburg PA
CBHW071347130626
46556CB00005B/2067

* 9 7 9 8 8 9 8 4 6 0 0 0 6 *